The Ultimate Guide

to Birthdays

By

Compass Star

*Secrets of Numerology to Occupation, Finance, Love, Health &
Things to Avoid & Suggestions | Your Complete Personology
Guide for Each Day of the Month*

TABLE OF CONTENTS

INTRODUCTION

What is the true meaning of a birthday horoscope that is hidden?

The date of birth is perhaps the most important number in a person's life. It is a reflection of a person's personality. The analysis of a person's birthday number also offers information about their future chances and specific information about their latent talents. Whether it's a job, finances, careers, love, or advice from others born on that particular day. Let's read it to find out who you're secretly like or to check your birthday horoscope.

Birthday Number 1
Born on the 1st Day of The Month

Personality is a ruthless entrepreneur with a gangster's heart. Have self-assurance and do whatever it takes to be a free-thinking, determined individual. Make every effort to become more self-assured. This is a frequent overall character feature until it is perceived as stubborn, not listening to someone who is dedicated, or doing something important. Many people are dissatisfied with this behavior since it is straightforward. This is a disadvantage that must be addressed as people become older. As people get older, pleasure takes precedence over success. However, be wary of what those born on the first day do; there are many contenders for very high competition. The more you work in a large organization, the more cautious you must be, and the risk of a lawsuit increases.

Occupation: Politicians can be famous for their health, which is ideal for merchants, teachers, and civil workers.

Finance: if you're looking for something innovative as a result, there is no need to gamble. may be drained So the priority should be to save. Before you consider investing for a secure financial future, consider the following factors.

Love: a constant affection that desires to do anything for the sake of the family.

Healthy: when you're near the end; your eyesight may be an issue, and your teeth may be deteriorating due to age.

Things to Avoid & Suggestions: People who can capture the hearts of those born on the 1st must-have similar behaviors. Have a clear vision of what you want to achieve in life. If you encounter someone who has the same personality as you. That person will be provided all of the time available to them to the utmost extent possible.

Birthday Number 2
Born on the 2nd Day of The Month

A person with a high sense of duty and perseverance has a personality. He is a person who places a high value on his friendships. a lonely individual He is a slacker, therefore he must concentrate on his buddies, as he has a large number of acquaintances but few of whom he knows. At the same time, he is obstinate and stubborn, yet he also listens to others. Have a strong sense of determination, ambition, and aspiration. As a result, those born on the second day are compassionate and polite. Always put your friends first in all you do. despite being genuine Then there's the fact that I'm a really intelligent person. Will go a long way in studying philosophy, literature, history, and archaeology.

Occupation: Historian or Work from home as a writer or researcher, however, the outcomes are influenced by emotions. Because people's moods are easily swayed.

Finance Take a rest and earn money. Know how to put it to good use. Understand how to collect. However, if you find something you like, you will use it without hesitation.

Love: There were a lot of people in the room, but you couldn't pick and choose. You have to feel disappointed and heartbroken before you can understand what true love is. You're having a love dream. People born on the 2nd of the month will find love in their mid-life or after 30 years of age.

Health: Allergies, gastrointestinal illnesses, and stomach

Things to Avoid & Suggestions: Creamy white or light green are the lucky colors, however black is not allowed. Warning: If you don't control your fury, you'll turn into something really cute.

Birthday Number 3

Born on the 3rd Day of The Month

People born on the 3rd day are more creative as a result of the number three's impact. possess leadership qualities It is a lucky number that represents women's fortune and love. Most essential, have faith in others. Consider the larger picture, organize yourself and others, and enjoy solving complex challenges. When it comes to trying new things, you're usually successful. A person who is inquisitive, educated, and has a special ability to evaluate and consider things properly.

Occupation: Become a professor. Lawyers, bankers, and even soldiers who serve as police officers are well-liked and respected.

Finance: Some people are worried about money, but they can eventually turn it around. As a result, there isn't much of a financial issue.

Love: Being a true lover is challenging, but saying I love you is much more difficult. Even if you're not a romantic person, if the noise can be controlled to some level, your love life will run smoothly.

Health: Inflammatory disorders such as cystitis, sinusitis, diabetes, and others. Women should be aware of disorders affecting the reproductive organs.

Things to Avoid & Suggestions: When contacting work or various enterprises, the lucky colors orange, red, should be worn. It is necessary to remove some anger for life to run smoothly.

Birthday Number 4

Born on the 4th Day of The Month

Mercury is the star of persons born on the 4th, resulting in a chatty person, negotiating, and moody. Personality can be inconsistent at times. It's good to be a hard worker, to enjoy work, to be a hard worker with a high sense of duty, to be serious about everything related to work, including relationships with friends or lovers. Expecting too much from others' actions and intentions, and getting too worked up with friends.

Occupation: Because it is someone who understands others, it is excellent for me as a speaker. Can persuade others with their words When friends encounter problems, they can also assist in totally resolving them. It's suitable to be a mentor, a thinker, a writer, a reporter, or an astrologer.

Finance: Even if you don't have much money, being a lucky person in finance will look for ways to create money. Even collaborations with anyone can work with you to create a reputation.

Love: This is love's flaw. Life is not easy; you will fall in love many times and maybe married twice.

Health Oral or dental disease can cause complications; therefore, you should take extra precautions

Things to Avoid & Suggestions: Sunday, Monday, and Saturday are lucky days for doing anything successfully

Birthday Number 5
Born on the 5th Day of The Month

Jupiter (5) influences a fussy purist. He was tall, well-proportioned, and smart. Careful execution has a wide range of benefits. Being a good advisor to others is a fantastic thing to do. Are eager to work or learn new skills, but I must confess that I am a stubborn individual. It's referred to as obstinate, and it has its justification. Dual personality refers to a set of manifestly contradictory habits. Accept what will happen, whether it must be fulfilled or disappointed, and is a person who is constantly encouraging, never giving up on issues or barriers.

Occupation: You are qualified to work as a teacher, a doctor, a nurse, a judge, or a lawyer who gives training. You'll be far ahead of the game. or operating alone or with a small group

Finance: Many people do not need to be concerned about money and they are a nearly middle-aged success, but there are always ups and downs since they must always support brothers and sisters.

Love: Because of the success of the job first, you might get married afterward. Importantly, they have been disappointed so many times that they have lost faith in love.

Health: Nothing to worry about, just a small headache. that results in the deterioration of the body Criteria for surgery 1 time in life.

Things to Avoid & Suggestions: Wednesday and Friday are excellent days for deal business.

Birthday Number 6
Born on the 6th Day of The Month

People born under the influence of the 6th astrological sign It has to be someone with a lot of love, desire, and charisma. white in nice condition If it's a man, he's tall and white (usually), and he's quite particular about his clothing. like to dress fashionably. The majority of people born on this day, regardless of the month, are flirty. It has to be attractive. Gentle and adaptable to any setting. Personal traits, such as the need for affection, the need to be cautious, and those who come to me with honesty or not.

Occupation: Professional artists in all professions, architects, tailors, hairdressers, celebrities, models, art teachers, or finance are all viable options.

Finance: Money is easy to get by and is put to good use. The majority will be swayed by their charm or attractiveness.

Love: Give priority to the people you care about rather than your sexual orientation. Even if the reality is fire, if someone has a partner who was born today, the one who started inciting sex first should be the one. Most of the time, there will be a lot of love and people will marry young.

Health: Be cautious of disorders of the uterus, liver, and kidneys, as well as stress-related diseases, and rest and take care of yourself.

Things to Avoid & Suggestions: Pink or orange are fortunate colors. To be successful, significant corporate deals should be made on Tuesday or Thursday.

Birthday Number 7

Born on the 7th Day of The Month

People born on the 7th have profound thoughts due to Saturn's influence. A profoundly secluded world is described as an introverted body. Has a mentality that is difficult to comprehend. The skin is reddish, rather dark, and the shape is tall and slender with long hands and feet. The face appears to be that of a sad individual. A person who enjoys trying new things. They are daring and prefer to learn from firsthand experience rather than from books, studies, or stories. If you don't want to do something, you'll cease doing it right away without informing anyone, a self-contradictory person. When it comes to making decisions, there are always forks on the road. You're undecided about whether to turn left or right. You're undecided about whether you'll follow society's standards or let go of your free spirit. This is a disadvantage, but a skilled person with good memory and exceptional clarity will overcome it.

Occupation: Careers aren't always willing to adapt or take risks. Bomber, Undertaker, Warden are all suitable occupations.

Finance: You have a steady cash flow and good fortune is always on your side. If you save and invest, you have a chance to become a billionaire.

Love: You can be a flirt at times. But you don't enjoy it when your lover flirts. You enjoy admiring people who are attractive and well-dressed. You, on the other hand, dislike it when your partner dresses up or dresses too handsomely.

Health: Walking with caution, joint pain, orthopedic knee pain, and stress are all things to consider.

Things to Avoid & Suggestions: On Sunday and Monday, may the force be with you. Try to buy the lottery on the day it is drawn; you might win.

Birthday Number 8
Born on the 8th Day of The Month

It's Myth Day. On this 8th day, individuals will be neat, everything must be correct... in terms of learning, accumulating knowledge, this star will be stable. Various kitchenware and things will be neatly organized. Dress, taste, courtesy, and demeanor are all excellent. If a good policy planner is interested in something, he or she must learn the fundamentals of that subject.

Occupation: Speakers, protestors, community leaders, lawyers, and politicians are all excellent choices.

Finance: Spend a lot of money, get a lot of money, and you'll soon run out of money, have no idea what to do with it, but be fortunate enough to have money to spend.

Love: Obstacles and disappointments abound, as well as problems with family life due to your changeable and unstable personality. Be wary of the love triangle.

Health: Tend to become ill frequently, frequently suffering from headaches, fevers, sleeplessness, and osteoarthritis. As a result, you should relax and exercise regularly.

Things to Avoid & Suggestions: Blessings to your parents, and remember to let the animal life feed the animals on Saturday, Sunday, and Monday, and you will have amazing success.

Birthday Number 9
Born on the 9th Day of The Month

A personality is a person who enjoys doing weird things, is only interested in strange things, is good-natured, enjoys laughing, enjoys having interesting adventures, and only stays still for a short period. Work hard, and insight can be so profound that some people are unaware of it. Think in terms of cause and effect, and like learning new things.

Occupation: Can do anything except work for the government, unless it's on a project or for a private company that gives solid advice. You have a gift for explaining things and narrating stories in a way that people can understand.

Finance: It's not about money to spend money on luxury; it's about clothes, food, eating, and living; you'll have to eat well, and you won't regret spending money on these things. Furthermore, donors are always willing to provide.

Love: There is a lot of affection, but it isn't enough to be serious. It appears that love is a major issue. It is preferable to be single rather than married because arguments are more likely to occur.

Health: Be wary of diseases that cause back pain, neck discomfort, and finger locks, as well as allergies, skin disorders, vision problems, and light allergies

Things to Avoid & Suggestions: Make it a point to meditate and make merit regularly.

Birthday Number 10
Born on the 10th Day of The Month

Uranus is in charge of people born on the tenth day, resulting in their yin and yang. Happiness, for example, includes suffering, as well as good and evil, white and black. It has been defined as a number that has no significance, leaving nothing, or changing, going wrong, and destroying the old by its nature. Personality has no way of knowing what you're thinking. You are too tranquil, whether you are unhappy or joyful. This is what this number means. It's referred to as a "very private universe." Intelligence can sometimes be too much for a person to be insane. Farsighted, with thoughts that the people around him cannot comprehend, yet always in a good mood and having a wonderful time. In business or issue solving, the edge is the leader.

Occupation: Energy scientist, pilot, trekker, medical professional, and explorer are all good choices.

Finance: Don't worry about your finances; no matter how much money you receive, you may not know how to put it to good use. Keep going until you lose track of how much money you have.

Love: You have a chilly and uncaring affection for each other, and you rarely express it. Quarrels are disliked by some people, while others are not. There's a chance you'll meet a wonderful lover. Come into existence, yet some stars can be split, thus being single is preferable to be married.

Health: Traveling should be avoided due to the risk of accidents, disease in the shadow, leg and foot irritation, and respiratory disease, thus smoking should be avoided. because there is a higher risk of sickness than others.

Things to Avoid & Suggestions: Participated in the construction of churches and temples, or created something for the public good. Indigo purple is a wise hue that will help you achieve your goals.

Birthday Number 11
Born on the 11th Day of The Month

A person with a particularly self-centered personality is referred to as a personality. On the outside, it's soft, but on the inside, it's hard. They don't have to speak again if they say no. The exterior has a lovely softness to it. It's intricate and difficult to comprehend on the inside. a someone who is imaginative Do whatever you want, relying primarily on your imagination and feelings. I despise being compelled to do something I don't want to do.

Occupation: Because you are ambitious, have clear goals in mind, and enjoy working. Government work was wonderful, but one had to be wary of obstinacy.

Finance: You can save and accumulate money even if you don't have much. You understand the worth of money because you are a person who understands it.

Love: There is never enough love, so be picky about who you love, make a lot of choices, and be cautious. People who don't love each other typically end up as partners in the end.

Health: Allergies, gastrointestinal disorders, and stomach difficulties are common, thus eating on time is essential.

Things to Avoid & Suggestions: You're a water elemental, you should wear pearls or white gemstones as jewelry since they bring stability to your life.

Birthday Number 12

Born on the 12th Day of The Month

The Sun's (1) and Moon's (2) influences collide and complement each other. So, like everything else in life, there are ups and downs. You are a gifted and open-minded individual who does not exploit others and does not enjoy being exploited. You're the type of person who speaks bluntly, leaving the listener feeling unsatisfied or hated, making you a less-than-friend, a number to be aware of obsessions.

Occupation: You have a lot of ambition. As a result, my professional goal is to be the owner of my own company. Beauty, risk gambling, and commercial jobs are all good options.

Finance: You are a luxury spender who isn't in desperate need of anything. Because you have a decent source of income.

Love: Monotony irritates him, as does having a strong sexual urge. If you have a heart for someone born on this day. Having to alter the location of sex and the posture of having sex regularly.

Health: Celiac illness is a kind of celiac disease that Abdominal discomfort, uterine spasms, and prostate cancer are all caused by a lack of veggies and regular exercise.

Things to Avoid & Suggestions: This effect is caused by the Sun and Moon's influence: white, cream, and gold. The bright yellow color heightens people's feelings of friendliness and compassion.

Birthday Number 13

Born on the 13th Day of The Month

Numbers 1 and 3 are adversaries, and when they come together, there is always something good and something evil that happens. Because you are incredibly attractive, have a soft heart, are honest, and like assisting people. However, there are moments when you have unusual thoughts and deeds, an awe-inspiring attitude, are serious, and believe in yourself; your flaw is being excessively optimistic. When you're in charge of learning, you're more likely to keep learning.

Some people, on the other hand, may only study halfway through.

Occupation: Art, government, and different crafts pique my interest. Work as administrative law or in a position that necessitates the use of language.

Finance: Money is constantly in and out of circulation. It's simple to generate money, to spend money wisely, and to spend a lot of money.

Love: You are a person who truly loves someone, hates anyone, really hates, and enjoys eroticism.

Health: Eye issues, kidney disease, and disorders of the internal organs are all common. Things to be aware of in the event of an accident or being struck by a sharp weapon.

Things to Avoid & Suggestions: Help people, help society. Vipassana practice and you will discover surprising things.

Birthday Number 14
Born on the 14th Day of The Month

The Sun's (1) paired with Mercury's (2) influence determines the fate of people born on the 14th (4). When they join forces, they urge life to rise to the grandeur of Number 1, Fire Element, and Number 4, Earth Element, keeping the fire burning unabated. There are germs because there is dirt to sustain them. Has an inventive spirit and a keen intellect. and the ability to recall specific information Excellent problem-solver You're a teacher, whining and methodical for a minute. You are a powerful and vivacious individual.

Encourages you to make the most of your existence.

Occupation: Any sort of self-challenging employment will do well, including reporter, journalist, mass media, television, and radio work.

Finance: You don't have to be concerned about money because you are a person who saves and spends wisely. Even if you don't have a large sum of money, you can still save comfortably.

Love: You are lovely, and many people fall in love with you, so you don't have to deal with love too much.

Health: Diseases such as knee discomfort, ankle pain, wrist pain, acid reflux, and stomach sickness should all be avoided, so eat on time.

Things to Avoid & Suggestions: Leaf green, earth tones, and blue are fortunate colors.

Birthday Number 15

Born on the 15th Day of The Month

It's a fortunate number with concealed power, allure, and allure that makes people fall in love with it. if the commander is courteous, passionate loves justice, such as beauty Luxurious, attractive, and appropriate for people of various socioeconomic levels. There will be individuals ready to lend a hand. You're a terrific speaker, persuasive, talented, caring, and attractive. The fact that I enjoy fighting is an advantage. Likes to overcome obstacles and make progress on their own.

Occupation: You're a politician, a governor, an executive, a merchant, and a musician, an artist, and a dramatist. It has a high level of personal appeal. As a result, it has gained popularity among those who have witnessed it.

Finance: In finance, there is a lot of luck. It's simple to get information about financial concerns. I'm not wealthy, but neither am I destitute, and I'm trying to make ends meet. You should be able to manage your finances well. Rather than spending money on yourself, spend it with friends or on vacation.

Love: Even if it's lovely, it's not particularly promising. for there will be love concealed Frequently, the person you love does not love you. Even if you don't love them, they will always adore you.

Health: Stress-related disorders, cancer, sexually transmitted diseases, and heart disease, including joint pain and bone pain in the knee joints, should all be considered.

Things to Avoid & Suggestions: Always be forgiving, practice meditation, and follow the commandments. You'll discover miracles if you look hard enough.

Birthday Number 16

Born on the 16th Day of The Month

The influence of Saturn is felt on Day 16, when the numbers 1 and 6 are put together to create the number 7, resulting in you being a person who has to deal with mainly unpleasant situations. There are numerous barriers to overcome, such as the desire to seek out new experiences, to explore, and to have a meaningful life. He is enthusiastic, yet he prefers to keep his opinions obscure.

Occupation: You are correct in stating that it is an issue of investment risk. Likes to do jobs that aren't typical of the villagers, and to do things that no one else does. As a result, careers are insecure. If becoming a soldier, police officer, governor, or politician gives you the potential to get to the top.

Finance: There are several occasions when this occurs. There isn't enough time. Financial flashing isn't always accurate. As a result, be cautious while spending a large sum of money.

Love: Because your love has gone through so much, you rarely trust anybody in love. Because you love someone deeply, it hurts a lot when your love isn't reciprocated. Believe me when I say that being alone is much better.

Health: Migraine headaches, surgery, or difficult-to-treat conditions such as cancer are all reasons to pay attention to your diet and exercise while remaining stress-free.

Things to Avoid & Suggestions: Allow yourself to heal from your traumatic past by forgiving yourself and meditating.

Birthday Number 17
Born on the 17th Day of The Month

People born on this day have a high intelligence that is simple to grasp and a tendency of assisting others, according to their horoscope. It appears like life is taking place in an unfavorable setting. In life, there are several challenges. Adult pressure, bullying, and being exploited by jealous individuals are all things that children face. That was disguised by merit; patience is required for all of them. What you should avoid is blindly trusting somebody or listening to something and believing it without question. If you're careful, you'll be able to accomplish achievements or goals that are tough to attain. However, I would caution you that the narrative should not be expected to produce huge results. monetary problems Do it now, and the money will come afterward.

Occupation: Appropriate for careers in politics, law, or speaking, as a speaker.

Finance: Money and gold are available without a shortage of hands. It's simple to locate. Spend your money wisely. People who utilize the money to spend more money on themselves to be happier.

Love: People born this day have a hard time falling in love. Because simply enabling those who are close to us to accept who we are is sufficient.

Health: You have a higher risk of stress, anxiety disorder, and alcoholism if you drink with it, so be cautious.

Things to Avoid & Suggestions: Keep donating and meditate often to keep your breath balanced.

Birthday Number 18
Born on the 18th Day of The Month

You take things seriously, which may be overwhelming at times, but the number 18 indicates the number of warriors who address difficulties with caution. Have a powerful, deep, and sensitive intellect yet can be quickly annoyed. Whether you're in a good or terrible mood, you're not going to wait. You can sometimes work or accomplish anything you want without feeling rushed or pressured. Don't be concerned; your skills are bursting with vitality.

Occupation: You are a multi-talented individual. You will like research and demanding, challenging jobs in particular. Scientists, chemists, and researchers will become well-known.

Finance: Your cash will be simple to locate, not due to a lack of hands, but because you have a huge heart and spend an infinite amount of money to care for those around you, you will be able to pay out fast.

Love: There is always separation when there is love. You must be very mindful of love since you seldom achieve your goals. Frequently disappointed because love makes life all too easy to be widowed.

Health: The majority of them are brought on by stress, lack of sleep, and insufficient rest. Keep an eye on your blood pressure and headaches.

Things to Avoid & Suggestions: You'll find light in your life if you meditate.

Birthday Number 19

Born on the 19th Day of The Month

Born this day, it entails total joy and success in life. Its effort mana is extremely high. Have a high level of tolerance for a wide range of circumstances. The obstacles that appear are like waves that come and go, never flinching at the events or problems that wash up on the beach. You are a caring individual who is self-assured and has a positive attitude toward others. When you're insulted, acting dignified is like pouring oil on a fire.

Occupation: Great opportunities abound in life. Always come in or have a compassionate elder to assist you, so whether you work for the government or a large private personal business, success is usually not difficult.

Finance: Fortunately, in terms of money, there is plenty of it to go around and spend on anything one desires.

Love: There might be love many times, flickering with passion, but true love has no life. Because it is a fire element number, it frequently causes issues in relationships.

Health: Avoid smoking and consuming unhealthy foods to reduce your risk of respiratory illness, heart disease, high blood pressure, and diabetes.

Things to Avoid & Suggestions: When a couple must also be conscious of their feelings. The prestige rubies or red gemstones are enhanced by jewelry.

Birthday Number 20
Born on the 20th Day of The Month

You are a very volatile individual with a high level of intelligence. clever and quick to pick up on other people's ruses A person with a huge heart who is capable of doing things. As a person with a good hunch, do something significant. Dare to think, dare to be a decent person in your surroundings. Quite delicate, but romantic You're adept at hiding your secrets, but you're also skilled at picking up on other people's. Learning about art is ambitious because you want others to recognize your talent.

Occupation: You might start a business on your own or engage in writing, lecturing, publishing, radio, or television.

Finance: The financial system is rigid. But it's enough to keep spinning, and it's not uncommon for affection to pay the bills. Not particularly lavish, but if you like something, you will purchase it without hesitation. As a result, the funds should be split into multiple portions.

Love: They keep coming in, but something isn't quite right. You're a fussy individual who isn't happy with just about anyone. You're always on the lookout for love until it's time to blend in. There isn't any other option.

Health: You should exercise to strengthen your immune system and avoid diseases caused by genetics or allergies.

Things to Avoid & Suggestions: Help others, forgive others, and keep meditating to cleanse your thoughts. Then you may discover that many ailments that exist are readily cured or that you may locate a professional to treat them.

Birthday Number 21
Born on the 21st Day of The Month

You are a very easygoing but dual-behavior person if you were born on the 21st. Two emotions are self-contained and modest on the outside. Can integrate into society on any level, has a large number of friends, and is a person who adjusts well to his surroundings. Keep meticulous records of the individuals you meet and the job you accomplish. Has a gift for persuading intelligent people, and she has a lovely and appealing appearance. However, on the inside, there is a tough person who can hide one's personality deftly, and external displays tend to mask one's actual sentiments from others. When it comes to becoming more definite, the soft sweetness will be extremely hardcore.

Occupation: Suitable for starting a small personal company and gradually expanding. or work in public relations and advertising You can also work as a tour guide in a foreign language, although this is not appropriate for government positions.

Finance: You are a frugal person who spends money sparingly and earns money with the freedom to do anything you want. However, the funds will be used for more personal reasons. So, for each sort of expenditure, attempt to divide your money into numerous portions. You may rest assured that you will never run out of money.

Love: Your relationship with your partner will begin as a friendship and will eventually lead to marriage. It appeals to a large number of individuals since it is pleasant. If you are married, though, you must work in addition to caring for your family.

Health: You can quickly acquire weight if you are freed. Disorders of the blood system, respiratory system, diabetes, lipids, and different skin diseases are all possible.

Things to Avoid & Suggestions: Make your hair look better to improve your luck. Don't pull your hair back to hide your face; instead, open it up to accept good fortune.

Birthday Number 22
Born on the 22nd Day of The Month

Let's take a look at two numbers now. The 22nd birthday is associated with a complicated personality. Like two persons trapped in one body, they like to fantasize and create castles in the air, which conceals the deceit behind the scenes. You are self-assured (stubborn), do not like to keep your feet still, and are always surprising others around you. Likes to try out new and unusual things. On the surface, you appear to be a powerful individual, but on the inside, you are hesitant and uneasy with your ideas, unsure if you are good-hearted yet very sensitive. It has the advantage of being compliant with the rules.

Occupation: Entertainment, singers, actors, publications, and writings are all possible options.

Finance: There are always more on the way, but not enough to fulfill demand. Be responsible with your money, capable of producing money, and willing to go above and above for your family. So it's a smart idea to reduce your purchasing requirements, and you'll save a lot of money in the process.

Love: You are a person who is concerned about the people around you and who adores his or her family. You are concerned about every one of them. Everyone is called to prioritize their family as the most important thing in their lives. Anyone who has such a relationship is regarded as extremely fortunate. However, don't be so concerned that you make the other person uncomfortable.

Health: Epilepsy, allergies, and stomach discomfort are more frequent in this population than in the general population.

Things to Avoid & Suggestions: Wear clothing in the colors cream, light yellow, light green, and blue. Silver should be used for accessories. Then there will be a new type of luck.

Birthday Number 23
Born on the 23rd Day of The Month

Suppose a man for partnerships with the opposite sex, this number is ideal. In matters of love, there is a powerful temper known as a womanizer that is tough to capture. Multiple ladies can be present at the same moment. You are a person who places high importance on love. When you meet someone, you like, you can expect them to give it their best. It's preferable to have a prominent adult assist a lady. as a consequence of which you will have a prosperous life, Some folks can also be flirty. It's OK if you're attractive and have a lot of partners. Habits in general seldom give up on anybody and enjoy winning at everything. When a group loses something and it's tough to persuade them to change their minds, it's excellent. It's awful when it's bad.

Occupation: You are well-suited for a profession as a government servant, military officer, police officer, technician, engineer, teacher, or nurse, and you can easily succeed in your chosen field.

Finance: Knows how to spend money wisely; has a lot, spends a lot, has a little, spends a little; and has an excellent savings account. If you divide the money in this manner. You'll have enough money to live comfortably.

Love: You can easily fall in love, yet loving someone older than you will benefit you.

Health: High blood pressure, diabetes, obesity, urinary tract illness, and problems with the reproductive system are all possible outcomes.

Things to Avoid & Suggestions: Work as a contractor in an eastern location. will be beneficial, and commercial discussions on Wednesday or Friday will be successful.

Birthday Number 24
Born on the 24th Day of The Month

It is a combination of good fortune, charm, and attraction for a man of love, whether dominant or subordinate. You are kind, romantic, and passionate about justice. Kindness and good manners toward others around you. Always willing to lend a helping hand to those in need without expecting anything in return. The drawback is that when it comes to personal information or your thoughts, you tend to remain quiet and not tell anyone. Influential people frequently assist them, implying that they must network with high-ranking members of society and hold a significant position.

Occupation: Art, business people, critics, travel employment, and specialist physicians are all good options.

Finance: You are fortunate in that you have individuals who are always willing to help you with your finances. Financially, it is not a problem. Anything that can be caught may be used to generate money. It is unquestionably not difficult to conclude one's life.

Love: You are a lovely individual who will attract the attention of others; you will fall in love with someone who truly cares for you and is romantic. Prepared to provide joy to your loved ones.

Health: Your health isn't great, and you're ill a lot. Even if you appear to be in good health, watch your food and lifestyle frequently.

Things to Avoid & Suggestions: Onyx or black stone jewelry should be worn. It will assist you in being healthy.

Birthday Number 25
Born on the 25th Day of The Month

Saturn, the planet of sorrow, difficulties, and life troubles, is represented by the number 25, which adds up to 7. As a result, persons born on December 25th face a variety of issues. Some difficulties must be tackled all of the time in life. You are a person who values freedom and wants to have their views, live a distinctive lifestyle, don't want to follow others, have high standards, and love and appreciate their friends. Creativity, a desire to learn new things, initiative, speed, and the ability to solve issues as they arise.

Occupation: Duties on a variety of mechanic jobs, including military and police work.

Finance: The financial situation is precarious. Although there are several methods to generate money, there are also numerous ways to waste money. As a result, money should be saved and costs divided into sections so that money may be used in an emergency.

Love: You are impatient and don't want to be perplexed; nevertheless, some individuals marry late or have a late marriage; thus, once married, you should remain calm and communicate with each other. Don't let your emotions get the best of you.

Health: Anxiety or stress-related disorders If you have had at least one surgery on your stomach or intestines, you should exercise frequently to relieve tension.

Things to Avoid & Suggestions: Merit should be given to persons with impairments, the elderly, and the color white, blue, or bright green should be used since it promotes charisma and business.

Birthday Number 26
Born on the 26th Day of The Month

It's a number that denotes long-term prosperity and stability. Have leadership qualities and know-how to handle your own life. A good all-rounder is a strong individual who can take control of any circumstance. Have empathy for others, be able to see other people's difficulties, and sympathize with friends or others in your environment.

Occupation: If a lawyer is involved, Work as a financial counselor or auditor in finance and banking. By leaps and bounds, the task will be completed.

Finance: You're a solid earner who's never short on cash, and you're even wealthy. Don't put your money into stuff you don't understand; it's easy to be scammed.

Love: You are a romantic who is concerned about the well-being of those close to you. However, be cautious since the flirt was silent and someone was approaching.

Health: Accidents involving water should be avoided. As a result, while going by water, make sure to have appropriate safety equipment. Because of the risk of chest, lung, and respiratory illness, you should not smoke at all.

Things to Avoid & Suggestions: Make a good case supporting animals. Muted hues, silvery grays, light grays, or clothes with beautiful but not showy patterns are all lucky colors.

Birthday Number 27
Born on the 27th Day of The Month

When the numbers 2 and 7 are put together, they equal 9, a lucky and protective number. You're a man who takes his life seriously. Honest, fair, but the effect of the Moon (2) and Saturn (7), when they coexist in the horoscope, makes the owner of this planet seem like a wretched person with sorrow in the heart, in addition to being a fortunate star. You're a quiet person who isn't very cheery but who keeps his or her troubles hidden. It's simple to consume, doesn't infringe on anyone's space, and isn't overly lavish. If some worry is removed, life may be extremely successful.

Occupation: Technicians, explorers, seamstresses, or employment in food and pastry carving or chief should all be considered.

Finance: You can always find a method to make money. Even if the task is tiny, you don't mind having money on hand all the time. There will be money, gold, and prosperity in the future. Your money will increase quickly if you invest more in assets.

Love: Love rarely goes as planned, and it's certainly not romantic. A couple may not see each other very often or live far apart.

Health: You're most likely suffering from amnesia. As a result, eat brain-boosting foods and exercise daily, or play mental games.

Things to Avoid & Suggestions: Making merit, rescuing animals, and practicing meditation are all good things to do. Try living in harmony with nature.

Birthday Number 28
Born on the 28th Day of The Month

You have a kind demeanor. Loves people easily but gets bored soon, has self-confidence, is content with life, is not overly rigid but frequently contradicts himself. It appears strong and ferocious from the outside. However, individuals are considered to be easily fooled and deluded on the inside, sensitive, and disturbed. You have a lot of feelings in your heart, but you don't always express them. Another bad behavior is refusing to accept the facts. Personality is clever and capable of quickly resolving issues.

Occupation: You should work in the fields of art, public speaking, and marketing materials. actor and news anchor.

Finance: You are an excellent money earner; yet, individuals sometimes find themselves in need of financial aid.

Love: Frequently encounter elderly couples that encourage and support one another. People who are not single, on the other hand, will become involved in a double love affair, and a love triangle will end in disappointment.

Health: You're most likely suffering from a bladder infection. sexually transmitted illnesses, for example, If the person is a guy, the prostate disease is a possibility. If a woman is at risk for uterine cancer.

Things to Avoid & Suggestions: There will never be a scarcity of money if you make merit with dogs regularly. You should be monogamous because else you risk getting a sexually transmitted illness that is both easy to contract and difficult to treat.

Birthday Number 29

Born on the 29th Day of The Month

You're the one who sticks out from the rest of the pack. multi-talented, creative, self-assured, rarely listens to others, does what you want, but always has to be right Life is full of disappointments, and we are continually suffering. Life appears to be brilliant on the surface, but it is dark on the inside. Many adversaries stood ready to strike, but they were unable to do so.

Occupation: Being a company owner or an innovator who has tried new things is frequently required.

Finance: Know how to make money foresight works for you. There is plenty of cash to go around. If you don't have any money, though, you should refuse to accept aid from anyone.

Love: Some people marry later in life, while others remain single for a long period. If you are married, you will be a one-sided person who bears a tremendous deal of responsibility for your family and loved ones.

Health: There's a risk you'll develop a migraine if you don't take care of your blood system. As a result, exercising and getting proper rest should not be a stressful experience.

Things to Avoid & Suggestions: Make merit for orphans and the old. Dark or gray is the fortunate color.

Birthday Number 30
Born on the 30th Day of The Month

You are a person who exudes self-assurance and has a decent heart. You are powerful, direct, and rarely lower your head to others. Mars (3) and Uranus (0) both have an influence. Be cautious of anything that occurs unexpectedly. The moment of glory arrives unexpectedly, and when it does, it must be handled with care. Work or business. Because you're so vocal, the allure vanishes when you say this. You dislike mingling with the masses. Because you're thinking, you don't enjoy the crowd.

Occupation: You'd be a good fit for a job as a teacher, historian, politician, or behind-the-scenes worker.

Finance: With your intellect and two hands, you can build your own body. As a result, there is enough money to spend if you know how to preserve it and not waste it. At the end of the day, there's a lot of gold.

Love: You have a lovely personality. And there's a lot to pick from. You enjoy difficult-to-obtain items because they provide a sense of accomplishment. If someone who likes someone born on this day attempts to seem as if flirting with them is difficult, it's understandable if they have to focus on you.

Health: Keep an eye out for illnesses of the circulatory system, dental disease, and oral disease.

Things to Avoid & Suggestions: Ask for pardon and assistance from your father and mother, talk softly, and remember to create merit with youngsters with impairments or the elderly.

Birthday Number 31
Born on the 31st Day of The Month

A person with great self-confidence is often a dreamer who enjoys building castles in the air. Stubborn dislikes stomping his feet in situ indicates that life is not at home and that he must always go out. You are a strong, resolute, and indomitable person who survives in any circumstance. You are modest, kind-hearted, love your friends, have a very excellent human interaction, a straight-talking person, and a strong, resolute, and indomitable person who survives in any situation.

Occupation: Appropriate for working in a small company Jobs at legal companies, printing houses, and selling office supplies are also possibilities. Whether it's selling stationery or medical gadgets or pharmaceutical substances.

Finance: A person who spends money on luxuries yet is nonetheless financially successful. Make money to spend without having to work for it. Even if you are a skilled money manager, you may save money while simultaneously putting it to good use. As a result, it should be separated into difficult-to-use savings and saves that require many processes before being utilized to have money to spend in the future.

Love: You must select a spouse who looks nice in all situations while choosing a mate. Making it harder to locate a spouse, late marriage, or being alone are all possibilities. Living in love is a lot when you're married, and it might make you or your partner uncomfortable at times.

Health: Be aware of osteoarthritis, knee discomfort, and back pain; thus, while lifting anything, it should be done correctly to avoid future issues, and you should consume healthy foods and exercise regularly to maintain your body strong.

Things to Avoid & Suggestions: Making merit with old people, asking for forgiveness from parents, and assisting them, can help your business flourish. When driving long distances, always check the engine first, stay alert, and avoid drinking alcohol. Black is a fortunate color.